SCRAPPED AND DISUSED LORRIES

CARL JOHNSON

AMBERLEY

First published 2020

Amberley Publishing
The Hill, Stroud
Gloucestershire, GL5 4EP

www.amberley-books.com

Copyright © Carl Johnson, 2020

The right of Carl Johnson to be identified as the
Author of this work has been asserted in accordance
with the Copyrights, Designs and Patents Act 1988.

ISBN 978 1 3981 0076 3 (print)
ISBN 978 1 3981 0077 0 (ebook)

British Library Cataloguing in Publication Data.
A catalogue record for this book is available from
the British Library.

Typesetting by Aura Technology and Software
Services, India. Printed in the UK.

Introduction

This book is about lorries that have either come to the end of their working lives or have been pensioned off to serve as yard shunters or even used as a source of spare parts to keep other lorries in service.

These have been captured on film by the author over a number of years in various states of decay from just off the road to total dereliction.

For many years, even after the First World War, a lot of dealers and scrapyards were dealing in ex-military vehicles and many hauliers took advantage of the vehicles available to start off in road haulage.

The Second World War also saw government surplus vehicles being sold off and again hauliers snapped up a lot of the vehicles, often with little or no recorded mileage.

Conversions were plenty, and often very innovative. Also available were a good reserve of spares for these motors, thus enabling them to carry on for many years.

In later years quite a number of vehicle 'breakers' saw a useful reserve stock of spares building up and many a haulier was grateful for the relative cheap availability of these, especially given the very competitive marketplace where rate cutting was always a threat!

These breakers were often also involved in the export of complete vehicles and the necessary spares; ex-British vehicles were in big demand in several foreign and Commonwealth marketplaces.

Nowadays there are still fleet disposal sales, often run by commercial auction specialists. Sometimes included in these sales can be the odd 'vintage' vehicle that may have been part of a fleet that has closed, or added to the auction to provide extra interest and attract a larger audience.

The photographs have been taken at various locations over the years when it was still possible to obtain access to some scrapyards and hauliers' premises.

However, there are others that were photographed in other surroundings including old quarries, hedgerows etc.. Where possible, the information as recalled is included in the captions.

It may be prudent to mention here that the photographs were taken a long time ago, and many of the vehicles will have long since disappeared. Obviously to try and seek these out now would result in a wild goose chase and no doubt possibly cause a certain amount of consternation, so could I respectfully ask for common sense to prevail?

Things now are very different with many hauliers, and scrapyards have to be aware and adhere to the rules and regulations of the health and safety executive.

Some of these are still amicable and with the right approach it is still possible to gain entry, even if it means having to undergo a brief pep talk and maybe even a health and safety video pointing out the rules and regulations. Once briefed and possibly equipped with a hi-vis jacket all you need is some stout footwear and a decent camera!

Over the years, preceding these rules it was still considered prudent by the author to make proper arrangements and to use common courtesy in obtaining permission to access premises, the times this was refused can be counted on one hand!

To all those that have allowed access, including the ones that thought it was a strange request to photograph lorries, myself and other enthusiasts convey our sincere thanks for their kindness.

It may have seemed strange at the time, but now it is good to look back at some of the scenes and vehicles that we enjoyed before times changed forever.

Having spent the majority of my life in and around the Staffordshire Moorlands it will be no surprise to the reader to see many of the photos in the book to have been captured in this area.

However, many trips on safari with other enthusiasts were undertook over the years, so some photos from these jaunts are also included.

The resultant photographs bring back many memories of makes and models before the onslaught and invasion of many foreign manufacturers and it is hoped the reader finds similar enjoyment in taking this look back in time.

The text and captions are all my own work and although I may have been interested in lorries all my life, we can all make mistakes. I apologise if any errors have crept in. If they have, they are entirely of my own making!

Acknowledgements

Over many years I have met lots of like-minded enthusiasts with a passion for lorries; far too many to mention individually. However, I must thank long time friends and colleagues that have given their time to join me on safaris and provided knowledge, both local to them and in other areas, namely Ian Moxon, George Barker, Malcolm Mortimer, Michael Marshall, John Andrew, Neil Matlock and Nigel Scaife. There may be others that have also contributed with tips and sightings, for this I am eternally grateful.

All photographs are from my own collection which takes up rather a lot of room, so I must give tribute to my wife, Kay, who patiently allows me to indulge myself in my hobby, often burying the dining room table under a mountain of paperwork and reference books etc.!

Thames Trader seen in a scrapyard at Middlewich, Cheshire. Although not used on the road the vehicle was used as a mobile aluminium smelter. The apparatus on the back includes a furnace and blowing equipment.

This Foden S21 'Mickey Mouse' chassis cab was one of the fortunate ones as it did get saved and was fully restored. I saw it in a dealer's yard in Sandbach, Cheshire, and as can be seen it is an ex-Imperial Chemicals Industry (I.C.I.) vehicle.

Although looking very sorry for itself, and having suffered some vandalism, this Scammell Pioneer was still used occasionally in a Welsh boatyard for winching vessels out of the water.

A rare ex-London Brick A.E.C. Mercury which was one of a number fitted with air suspension and a cab with 'suicide' doors. Again, this was one of the lucky ones as it was fully restored to original condition and livery.

At the end of its working life, this Foden S36 six-wheel tipper used to run out of local quarries in the Stoke-on-Trent area. It was parked in a yard awaiting its fate when photographed, judging by the condition it had not long been retired.

Stoke-on-Trent registered Dodge four-wheel tipper that was run by a Mr Gurney (owner driver) out of Croxden Gravel, Freehay, Staffs. After the owner retired the lorry was parked up behind a nursery, where it was tracked down by the author for a photo not long after it had disappeared.

En route to an evening vehicle event at Thornes Park, Wakefield, the author and a fellow enthusiast stumbled across this reasonably straight Bedford 'O' type somewhere in the region of Denby Dale. Its ultimate fate is unknown.

This is the remains of a Sentinel lorry that was stored in a yard in Cambridgeshire. With the underfloor engine and a bench seat in the cab they were popular as brewers' drays. This one was used as a source of spare parts for the restoration of another such vehicle.

A Foden FG six-wheel chassis cab that was one of many Foden vehicles stored in an enthusiast's yard in Cambridgeshire. The yard was also a useful source of spare parts for most Foden models. Luckily a number of the vehicles from this yard have survived into preservation.

This fine S20 Foden with lovely enclosed tank bodywork was new to the Albion Sugar Co. as fleet number 56. Fortunately, this particular vehicle was restored to its original livery. The vehicle to the right is a Foden S21 'Mickey Mouse' tractor unit.

Tucked away in a corner of an enthusiast's yard was this Foden S21 eight-wheel flat that at one time was in the Rank Hovis McDougall (R.H.M.) fleet. Sporting the Hovis brand headboard, it sat quietly awaiting its fate.

Foden FG 6-wheel chassis cab. An ex-army vehicle, it was re-registered with a civilian number and did eventually undergo a full restoration.

Very little is left of this B.M.C (Austin/Morris). It had survived for a good number of years in a Stoke-on-Trent hauliers' yard as a useful store. The demountable body on the back harks back to the years when meat was transported in this way.

When the author was an apprentice mechanic, this Albion Reiver, fleet number 41 in the Shirley's Transport operation, was a flat platform lorry on general haulage. Later on it had this tank fitted and was used to convey pottery clay in liquid form (slip) on local work around the potteries.

Seen in a Stoke-on-Trent scrapyards holding area. This Bedford O Type had come from a local company pending a decision to scrap, or maybe be sold on into preservation. As far as the author is aware it did not survive.

The sad remains of an A.E.C. Mammoth Major Mk V. It was used in the H. Tideswell's fleet of Kingsley, Staffs, before being pensioned off and used as a store. The owner moved house and the vehicle was recovered by Tideswell's and is seen here in their Cheadle, Staffs yard.

This Atkinson Defender eight-wheel bulk tipper was found on some spare ground in the Swadlincote, Derby, area. It was spotted one day when passing through and it looked in reasonable order. However, it was not taxed so presumably she had worked her last.

Having stood in this position in the Staffordshire Moorlands for many years this Albion recovery vehicle was eventually purchased for preservation. However, as far as is known it has not yet been completed. It is hoped it will again see the light of day as it is comparatively rare.

Ironically, this Foden S20 four-wheel tipper, Ex-Coppenhall scrap metal merchants from Sandbach, was in fact parked up out of use in a Sandbach dealers' yard. The yard was cleared many years ago and has been built on, it is not sure what happened to the lorry.

This Morris FFK survived a number of years as a useful yard crane in the ownership of a Stoke-on-Trent fairground family. Located for a number of years in their workshop yard it has not been seen now for a long time.

A number of scrapyards specialised in the disposal of ex-British Road Services and this one, which has long since been cleared out, was at Oadby in Leicestershire. In the photograph can be seen an A.E.C. Mammoth Major Mk III eight-wheeler with a Leyland Octopus on top!

London-based Waxed Papers had run this Thornycroft Trusty eight-wheel integral van. However, the fact it found its way to the Oadby scrapyard seems a bit odd, unless it had initially passed through the parent company in Hertfordshire.

Here we have an ex-Pickfords Heavy Haulage Atkinson Venturer. It had been purchased, as seen here, by a Cheadle (Staffs) garage proprietor and later on was fitted with heavy recovery gear, winch etc. Used for a number of years it later on passed into preservation.

Amazing what can be spotted when off the beaten track, or in this case off the back of a canal boat! While on a canal boat holiday this B.M.C FFK was seen at the back of a small boatyard presumably using the gantry apparatus to lift vessels in and out of the water. A steady hand was needed for this shot!

Back to Oadby for this one, and we have an ex-London Brick Albion, the faded roundels on the cab front depicted a logo of Phorpres Fred, which related to the brick manufacturing process of four press!

This B.M.C large Luton furniture van has long since disappeared, the construction of the 'Potteries Way' through Hanley, Stoke-on-Trent, signalled its demise. Interesting to note is that the vehicle was actually forming part of the company perimeter fence!

Austin WF recovery vehicle seen in Longton, Stoke-on-Trent, parked in a side street. There was a small garage nearby so it may be assumed it belonged to them, however as often the case when parking anything in the open it had unfortunately suffered from some vandalism.

An interesting shot, an ex-London Brick Company A.E.C. Mercury with an identity crisis! Sporting an E.R.F. badge it has on the platform the remains of a Sentinel steam lorry cab. The horse looks totally disinterested!

Having stood for many years in a yard at Uttoxeter, this Dennis Max was slowly rusting away and would have possibly been a source of spares for other vehicles. The yard was cleared a long time ago and there now stands a Little Chef restaurant on the site.

Mountford Brothers from Stoke-on-Trent ran this Scammell Rigid 8 for a number of years on steel movements from the Shelton steelworks, often with a bogie under long lengths of girders. Luckily it was purchased for preservation and can be seen on the rally circuit in the W. J. Riding livery.

Foden S80 tractor unit of Heygates the flour millers. Having been used as a shunter after coming off the road it eventually came to the end of its useful working life. Heygates are still in business to this day.

Nestling in the Staffs Moorlands countryside I was tipped off about this Seddon Mk V. After a little detective work, I located it and got the photo. Another vehicle which originated in Stoke-on-Trent and had been in use with a coal merchant.

Another B.M.C Luton furniture van, this time it's clear to see it's an Austin. I captured this by poking my lens through a fence off a public footpath many years ago in the Loughborough area!

This Leyland Beaver was originally registered in Newcastle upon Tyne; however, I believe it was collected by a Staffs enthusiast from Lincolnshire. The vehicle was to be used as spares, and the pallets mounted on the chassis also contained various Leyland bits and pieces.

Many years ago, there used to be general auctions at Congleton Cattle Market in Cheshire. This Mk V Seddon turned up on a low loader from a Sandbach dealer. Although it looked a little tired it was complete and on the day the seller actually started the lorry up. The Perkins engine sounded very sweet!

Over from Great Yarmouth, this A.E.C. Mammoth had been purchased from its original owners by a Staffordshire company with a view to restoring it. The trailer is detachable, but it is classed as a flexible six-wheeler. As far as is known it still awaits restoration.

A.E.C. Mammoth Major eight-wheel bulk tipper, photographed in Lincolnshire. Somewhere along the line it gained a Leyland front grille, a not uncommon practice as these parts were interchangeable on the Sankey Ergomatic cabs as fitted to Leyland, Albion and A.E.C.

In Tideswell's yard in Cheadle, Staffs, were these two A.E.C. Mammoth Major eight-wheelers which did in fact still run. They had been used on Herman Tideswell's farm to collect hay and for many years stood in a field being run off on an incline to start!

Cossington Commercials in Leicestershire were an E.R.F dealership. Quite how this ex-Murphy's Foden S20 tanker ended up there is anyone's guess, however years ago most dealers were happy to take vehicles of any make in part exchange.

This Thames Trader fuel tanker stood in this position for many years in the small village of Bosley on the Staffs/Cheshire border. It was something of a landmark, but only a couple of years later the small filling station was demolished and the Trader had disappeared.

One of the many ex-Health Authority Leyland Beaver X-ray vehicles, which, due to their limited mileage, gave long service. Quite a number found their way into preservation including this one that was seen waiting to be shot blasted before restoration started.

This A.E.C. Mammoth Major started life as an R.A.F. six-wheel aircraft refueller. It was purchased and converted to an eight-wheel tipper by an owner driver who used it on the Croxden Gravel contract, seen here after coming to the end of its useful life quietly awaiting its fate. The unusual drivers screen was fitted at the time of conversion due to the driver being a tall person!

An ex-Bassett's of Tittensor A.E.C. Mercury. It had been used on internal duties at the Croxden Gravel Quarry in the spun concrete pipe works. It had certainly suffered an arduous life before finding its way to a local haulage yard when the pipe works closed.

Originating from Driffield, Yorkshire, this Commer Maxiload was captured on film at the Klondyke Steam Centre, which is the home of the Staffs and Cheshire Traction Engine Club. Every year they had an open day and this vehicle, as far as known, was owned by a member that had other Commer vehicles.

Two Albion four-wheelers in the holding area of a Stoke scrapyard. The vehicle on the left, which dated from 1970, was interesting as it is actually a four-wheel drive and had been used on road construction sites as a fuel bowser. The one on the right had also been used as a bowser and is probably an ex-Shell motor.

Reputed to be a heavy haulage double drive tractor from the famous Sunter's of Northallerton, this lorry had been converted to a recovery vehicle. Having had the bodywork removed it had been put out to grass in an operator's yard. Of interest is the notification on the door stating that it had been 'graded' by Wreckers International.

This Morris FFK was new to a builder in Stoke-on-Trent. It was sold on and was used as an internal vehicle at Wood Treatment in Bosley to transport wood products such as sawdust, shavings and wood waste. It retained its original livery throughout.

Yet another ex-Health Authority Leyland Beaver that had been a mobile X-ray van. These did actually pull trailers during their working life. This one is seen having been purchased for spares, the lead-lined box van had already been stripped and the actual x-ray machine is still in situ.

A K-Series Dodge, which at the time was in use at the now defunct Hughes Concrete works in Leek, Staffs. Judging by the colour it may have been at one time running on the Croxden gravel contract, the paint was actually supplied by Croxden to most of their haulage contractors.

The old Brittain's paper mill site in Cheddleton, Staffs, saw a number of small businesses operating from this rather large site. Harrison Plant had presumably used this S80 Foden eight-wheel tipper on site work judging by its condition.

Leyland Lynx tractor unit that looks to be an ex-Esso vehicle. This too was seen on the industrial estate that is now on the Brittain's Paper mill site at Cheddleton. It had been used on site to shunt trailers around and may have been retired when the photo was taken.

Second generation Leyland Marathon 2, which was found on some wasteland near the main railway line in Stone, Staffs. This was spotted when on a Euston–Stoke train and the author managed to track it down at a later date! Ex-Howard-Tenens, it had suffered some accident damage and may have been used as a source of spares as there was another Marathon nearby.

In the same yard as the previous photo was this Scammell Crusader, however it is badged as a Leyland which indicates that it had more than likely been a military version. The crane on the back is certainly in army green paint but the cab looks suspiciously like its off an ex-Econofreight vehicle.

It's amazing what can be found tucked away if you have a keen eye. Very often you can stumble across vehicles like this Commer 'Maxiload' livestock vehicle that was spotted on a farm on the Derbyshire border. The farmer was only too pleased, if a little perplexed, to allow a photograph.

With a Birmingham registration number this B.M.C was another vehicle spotted while out and about. Its origins were not known, but it sports a Willenhall cab that was also fitted to other marques including E.R.F, Dennis and Guy.

Thornycroft Sturdy, which was seen at a haulage contractors' yard pending restoration, had been purchased along with another such vehicle. Unbelievably although purchased from different locations they both turned out to be from the same operator!

The remains of an Atkinson eight-wheeler in chassis cab form that was found on a property tucked away in the Derbyshire countryside. There were other vehicles in the yard in similar condition and this one had more than likely been purchased for spare parts as the owner operated a tipper on local quarry work.

Not a lot was left of this Thames 4D which was found partially under cover. It was in a barn off the beaten track on a derelict farm and one wonders why the chassis was protected from the weather rather than the cab!

Again, another derelict farm and another find was this Foden S80 tractor unit. Not much could be established about its owners or indeed its history. A lot of the identity had been covered over and maybe the headlamps had been removed as replacements for another such vehicle as to buy new ones was quite expensive!

On the same farm, and next to the Foden in the previous photo, was this ex-Shell Scammell Trunker Mk II. With the stylish Michelotti cab, these were a popular choice with several fuel companies. Whether this had seen any life with a consecutive operator is pure conjecture, but it had received a quick coat of paint over the original livery.

In what is often termed as 'hedgerow condition' this Bedford TA had been mentioned to the author by an acquaintance. Having been given a rough idea as to where to find it, an investigation soon had the old vehicle facing the camera. Alas now long gone!

Blue Circle Cement is a brand name still in use, however the nice livery depicted on the vehicles is now a thing of the past; a pity as can be seen in this Foden S21 'Mickey Mouse' the vehicles did look rather well. This one finished its days as a dust collector on internal work at the Cauldon plant, near Waterhouses, Staffs.

Notching back again to the derelict farm here we have yet another out of use Foden tractor unit, albeit this time an S83. We can see some identification on this one. The Bollington address in Cheshire had a connection with the owners as they had a property there.

Another Ergomatic cab with an identity crisis! This A.E.C Mandator tractor unit is fitted with a Leyland grille with a Lynx badge. Unfortunately, these Sankey built cabs were renowned for rust and many suffered an early grave, however it was not unknown for some vehicles to be fitted with the later T45 cab.

On the side of the A5 in Cannock, this Bedford QL four-wheel drive recovery vehicle stood for quite a while. Needless to say, after stopping to photograph it one day it disappeared soon after. At least it got captured on film.

All-wheel drive vehicles were always popular with recovery operators. This one was originally a 6 x 6 gritter for the Highways Agency. It made a useful recovery vehicle and was used for a number of years by a garage in Leek, Staffs. Since then the business has diversified and only has a filling station and garden centre on site.

David Harber from Longton, Stoke-on-Trent, at one time was known as a lime spreading merchant, later on he was involved as far as is known with canal boats. This ex-Mitchells & Butlers 'Chinese six' Bedford TK had been fitted with a beaver tail body and winch but had, by the time of the photograph, found its way to the same garage in Leek as the previous shot.

Recovery vehicles come in all shapes and sizes, and today it is a very specialised operation. Years ago, things were different and this Guy Big J4t in the Moss and Lovatt fleet had a concrete block over the fifth wheel to give traction when on breakdown towing work.

Another Guy Big J4T tractor unit was found in a Staffordshire hauliers' yard with its Motor Panels cab quietly rusting away. Keeping it company were several other makes of vehicles that have all now been cleared from the yard.

Talking of Motor Panels, seen here is another version of the cab fitted to this Seddon four-wheel tipper. The vehicle had long been off the road but was at the time used internally at Twyford's bathrooms factory in Etruria, Stoke-on-Trent. Twyford's had other factories and were a major player in the sanitary ware market.

Also in Twyford's at Etruria was this Leyland Super Comet, this too was engaged on internal work. The vehicle can be seen under the conveyor that carried waste clay out of the factory. Judging by the waste on the body the positioning was not always spot on!

This Leyland was among a number of such vehicles found at a garage in Derbyshire. Was it originally an eight-wheeler Octopus with the second steering axle removed? Or is it a genuine six-wheel Hippo? The cab looks a little like it may have been a Shell vehicle.

In the same location as the previous image, this Leyland Comet was somewhat rare as it had the Bonallack cab. However, these cabs did retain the standard front grille panel which was often referred to as the 'mouth organ'. It is not known if this vehicle actually survived into preservation.

A very complete Thornycroft Sturdy chassis cab that had been bought for preservation back in the 1990s. Originating in Shropshire the vehicle had crossed two county borders to end up residing in Derbyshire. Again, it was well off the beaten track!

Still in Derbyshire the author came across this Seddon Mk V four-wheel lorry that had at one time been with the Post Office. The Royal Crown can be made out on the cab door. This is another vehicle whose outcome is not clearly defined.

This really is a sad sight, an-ex-British Road Services Leyland Octopus '22' cab which had been stripped of most of its driveline components by a dealer. Once those had been removed, the chassis was considered to be of no further use. It was then placed with a number of other vehicles in a remote field to slowly decay.

A rough-looking ex-military Bedford with a scow end tipper. It was seen in a field one day when passing on the nearby road in the Derbyshire Dales. Seeking out the owner proved rather easy and access was allowed to take the photograph.

A very battered A.E.C 'Dumptruk', this was keeping company with the Bedford seen above. Again, it is fitted with a scow end tipping body. Due to the heavy nature of the work these had to do there are not many left.

A showman's yard in Sussex was the location of this A.E.C Mercury which the author stumbled across almost by accident. As always, a polite request resulted in the photograph being taken and kept for posterity. This may have been an ex-B.R.S parcels vehicle as it does have shades of green showing through the red paint.

Quite a rare sight in the UK was the Barreiros or 'Spanish' Dodge. A Chrysler subsidiary the factory was based in Madrid. This tractor unit had been used as a shunter by a plant operator over the Staffordshire border in the town of Ashbourne.

This lorry was really hard to find, a friend had told the author about it and after a lot of searching up in the Cheshire hills I managed to find it. It is an ex-London Brick Albion and as seen in a previous photo the Phorpres Fred roundels can still be made out.

Languishing in an old hauliers' yard was this Commer 'C' Series tractor unit that had been used, along with others in the yard, on the carriage of empty metal drums. Scammell automatic couplings were fitted to most of the vehicles due to the lightweight but bulky loads.

This little Dennis had at one time been used for the carriage of Gyproc which is a brand of plasterboard. It is highly likely that the vehicle had been painted in the customers livery by the haulage contractor who was based on the Staffs/Derbyshire border.

Another vehicle with a Scammell automatic coupling was this Thames Trader tractor unit. This too had been used on the metal drum work. Just to the left can be seen the nose of a Scammell Scarab three-wheel unit that were very popular with railway companies and had possibly been used to shunt trailers in the yard, or maybe for spares.

A now closed scrapyard in the Staffs Moorlands revealed this Thames Trader four-wheel tipper that had been used for collection purposes. Of interest is the Morris Minor pick-up in the back of the body.

Parked up after giving excellent service was this A.E.C Mercury which was found in a yard at Chickerell near Weymouth. Chalker's also ran an ex-fire appliance which had been converted to a furniture van. The front panel in the Luton van on this one hinged to allow the cab to tilt.

Found in a field near Macclesfield was this ex-R.H. Stevens E.R.F eight-wheel platform lorry. It had been robbed of its engine which was fitted to another lorry. This cab is the 8LV cab as fitted to the later E.R.F LV range but is not to be confused as an A Series which had different chassis engineering.

Also, in the Macclesfield area was this 'Chinese six' recovery vehicle that had one time been in the fleet of A. Brown of Connaught Street, Tunstall. Presumably at one time it was on the general haulage fleet before being converted for recovery work, quite how it ended up in this yard is not known. Browns are still in business to this day.

Slowly returning to nature many years ago in a Hertfordshire scrapyard was this E.R.F ex-B.R.S parcels box van. It was fitted with the Willenhall all-steel cab which unfortunately has suffered the ravages of time. Also the van body has collapsed within itself.

Phorpres Fred again shows himself in the roundels on the front of this ex-London Brick A.E.C Mercury. This too was in a Hertfordshire scrapyard and shows how vehicles deteriorate once left outside. The vehicle has probably long since gone as there has been some clearance on the site.

A '22' cab Leyland Beaver tractor unit that was well tucked away in some undergrowth with nature slowly taking over. Although in poor condition, it was reasonably complete and would have been a valuable source of spare parts.

Not a great number of these vehicles have survived into preservation. It is a Scammell Handyman Mk I which has seen its 'squashed doughnut' front grille panel removed. This cab was designed by Scammell, whereas the next generation Mk II and Mk III featured the Michelotti cab.

Another vehicle that had been taken out of service and pensioned off to the scrapyard was this E.R.F eight-wheel bulk tipper. Still very complete at the time, it wouldn't have been beyond a full restoration, however as the saying goes 'you can't save them all'.

Featuring the later Michelotti cab with oblong headlights was this Scammell Routeman Mk III. It looks to have an insulated body fitted which would have been for use on tarmac deliveries. It was minus the engine and the author had in fact refitted the front panel prior to taking the photograph!

Maybe this Atkinson and the one behind had provided a pair of windscreens for a restoration project as both are missing! What looks to be an ex-Texaco tractor unit is in the foreground, while the other is unidentified but does have the word 'Precision' on the headboard.

A.E.C Mammoth Major which looks like an ex-Bituminous Road Facilities vehicle was seen in another contractor's yard in Exeter. Fitted with a tar emulsion tank, these vehicles were favoured to spread the tar as they could maintain a slow speed with decent engine revolutions.

With the white band around the middle this looks to be like an ex-North Western BRS vehicle. The Motor Panels cab is typically showing signs of rust and unfortunately the windscreen has been smashed, which would allow the weather to further deteriorate this Seddon 32-4 tractor unit.

A Bedford KM with the distinctive double front bumper (although damaged) was another tar tanker which was in a yard in Exeter. Not many six-wheel KM lorries were built and this one had lingered on due to the nature of its work resulting in low mileage.

The remains of an E.R.F with the V-Type cab that was in a yard in the town of Sandbach, Cheshire, where it was built. It was minus its engine and other parts and it probably had a Gardner five- or six-cylinder engine which would have given it simply either a 5.4 or 6.4 model code.

A.E.C Mandator tractor unit which, although looking rather rough, was at the time still in use as a yard shunter in a Devon produce merchants' yard. The missing driver's door may have in fact aided the driver by saving a few minutes when changing trailers!

This Commer 'C' Series was found languishing on an old airfield in Derbyshire. It was in a compound with other scrap and out of use vehicles. Devoid of any identification other than the nickname 'Nellie 2' it had seen use as a recovery vehicle.

Another recovery vehicle that had seen better days was this Thames Trader that was seen in a yard down in Devon. The company was an offshoot of the previously seen produce merchants A.E.C Mandator. The Trader was originally going to be restored, however the vandalism that was quite severe may have halted the idea.

In the corporate livery of the time, this ex-E.R.F Limited tractor unit had definitely had its day. Stripped of various parts it was found in a Stoke-on-Trent haulier's yard in this sad state, and presumably has long since gone.

Now this would take some rescuing, a Scammell tractor unit which was still showing signs of its previous owner – A.E. Parr, Civil Engineers of Westbury, Wilts and London. As this was found in a Hampshire yard it would have come from Westbury. As far as it is known they only had offices in London.

Complete, but suffering the ravages of time, this Thames Trader four-wheeler was in the yard of its original owner down the leafy lanes of Hampshire. It was actually one of two that had been put out to pasture.

A pair of B.M.C FFK Luton vans in a Staffordshire scrapyard. The Austin on the left was from the now defunct Longton Group. It had been in the Knight and Riley International (removal and shipping division) and was actually being used along with the one on the right to store spare parts.

With nature slowly but surely taking over, this Mk V Seddon was certainly well beyond any rescue attempts. It lay in a Newcastle scrapyard and was completely devoid of any means of identification. The registration just visible on the platform was actually attached to an Albion number plate bracket.

A very early Morris Commercial CS11 from the 1930s. This example was found in a scrapyard near Shrewsbury that has long since been cleared. Typical of a wooden frame cab it was falling apart but quite a number of the metal panels were still intact. The name on the door reveals its origins.

Found in a showman's yard this E.R.F KV had long since been on the fairground circuit. Parked up in a yard it was, as a good number of van-bodied vehicles get used as, a store. However, the vehicle did eventually get scrapped.

A rarer version of the Morris FFK was this one with what is thought to be a Homalloy cab. Registered in Luton, Beds, it has been suggested that the vehicle was used by Her Majesty's Stationery Office. Quite how it found its way to a Staffordshire scrapyard is a mystery. However, the company did purchase a lot of vehicles at government surplus sales.

A temporary resident at a well-known Staffordshire dealers' yard, this Austin K2 originated with an operator in Banbury. Known as a 'Birmingham Bedford' this six-cylinder petrol-engined chassis cab was moved to pastures new, maybe as a source of spares for another of the same type?

S39 Foden eight-wheel tipper that was spotted many years ago on wasteland in the Streetly area which is part of the West Midlands conurbation. The colours look very much like it had been with Pioneer Concrete, either as a company vehicle or a contractor. Its registration number heralds from Barnsley.

Next to the S39 in the previous shot can be seen the beat up, vandalised remains of a Foden Haulmaster. Reduced to chassis cab form it was no doubt destined for the scrapyard. Some wag has penned the 'OUCH' remark on the front cab panel!

A blast from the past is this Leyland Buffalo tractor unit that was in the colours of The British Steel Corporation. It was actually parked in the graveyard as it was known at Bassett's Roadways in Tittensor, Staffs, before the big clearance was undertook.

Another Leyland Buffalo tractor unit which was looking a little tired. However, it was still being used to shunt trailers around a yard over in Norfolk. Its origins were unknown as at the time there was no one around to ask.

Something of a hybrid was this crane that had found its way into a collector's yard in Cheadle, Staffs. The front end is the remnants of a Blue Circle Cement vehicle and has flecks of yellow paint showing. The rear end bogie complete with crane may have been of military origin.

A Foden Haulmaster eight-wheel chassis cab that the author found in this rather vandalised condition in a yard in Rugeley, Staffs. It was one of a number of vehicles that had long since served their last duty in revenue earning service.

Fleet number 105 of Shirley's Transport was an ex-Royal Navy six-wheel Bedford KM that was refurbished to join the tanker division. It also received a new Staffordshire registration number but actually saw little service before being parked up.

What was probably the rarest vehicle in the Oadby scrapyard was this Rutland tractor unit. It was ex-G.L. Baker of Southampton, who had in fact ran a number of Rutland vehicles. Another ex-Baker Rutland was known to exist in the parent company's scrapyard in Hertfordshire.

An Atkinson Borderer tractor unit that had the addition of a sleeper 'pod' fitted. It would have been very cramped in there and a long way away from today's vehicles which have far better facilities. By the looks of the badge on the grille it may have had a Rolls-Royce engine.

Ex-National Coal Board Foden Haulmaster six-wheel tipper which was seen when on a visit to an operator in Leicestershire. The days of N.C.B. have long gone but the livery will be remembered well by many people.

Fitted with a heavy front bolster, which would have been for the carriage of long lengths of steel or even timber, this 'bow front' Atkinson eight-wheel flat platform lorry also served as a store for spare wheels and tyres and even an Atkinson cab.

Ex-Craddock Brothers of Coven Heath, Wolverhampton (fleet number 7). This vehicle was apparently an eight-wheel chassis that had been cut down to make this double drive tractor unit. Of interest is the double skinned 'tropical' cab roof. This too had found its way to an enthusiast's yard, but its fate is unknown.

With single headlights this looks to be an Austin WE model. However, it seems to have had some form of modification as the front grille bars are quite different from the standard version. The vehicle was seen at Astley Green Colliery a number of years ago, presumably as an exhibit.

Slowly being encroached by undergrowth this E.R.F eight-wheel box van had been in use on the fairground circuit. Sporting an Irish registration number its origins are unknown but here it was in an old yard in the Greater Manchester area.

At one time run by an owner driver on Staffordshire quarry work, this Foden S80 was found in a yard having come to the end of its working life. Showing no road fund licence, it was, however, in pretty good condition. Nowadays it would no doubt be worthy of preservation.

Another company that is no longer with us. W&J Wass (Sandford Hill Haulage) of Longton, Staffs, had this Guy Big J4T in use as a yard shunter. The company for many years specialised in the distribution of pottery from local 'potbanks' to all parts of the UK.

Spotted one day tucked away in a yard in Kidsgrove this A.E.C Mercury looked to be an ex-London Brick Company vehicle. By the looks of it there had been a certain amount of restoration work carried out. However just a few years later it had disappeared, so the outcome is unknown.

Not a lot is left of this unidentified Atkinson Borderer tractor unit. It was languishing in a Cheadle scrapyard which later on had a clear out to introduce more modern stock. Chances are it was scrapped for good!

Another train journey for the author and another spot! This S83 Foden was in use on internal work on an old colliery site where the waste was being screened. A bit of detective work resulted in tracking it down and, after some gentle persuasion, the foreman allowed access for the photo.

Typical of what some haulage companies did with certain vehicles, this E.R.F 54G originally had the earlier LV type cab but was re-cabbed with the later 7LV, which was on the A Series range. Confusion often arises with such conversions, this lorry was in McGuinness's scrapyard in Stoke-on-Trent, another yard since closed.

Foden Haulmaster chassis cab ready for the chop at McGuinness's scrapyard. The Haulmaster was a popular choice for tipper operators and this was once such a vehicle. Standing away from the main business at the top of the yard it is no surprise to see someone has borrowed the Foden script badge!

This 'Chinese six' E.R.F tipper was new to Llewellyn and was reputedly built like this to order. It later went to Robinsons of Rushton but when seen here it was out of use in the small village of Meerbrook. It certainly had a long life.

Scammell Routeman Mk III chassis cab. This was in a hydraulic specialists having had its 'Big Bite' refuse body removed to be mounted on its replacement, which was actually an E.R.F. The operator originally started as a scrap dealer but expanded into waste disposal.

Cheshire registered Foden S83 eight-wheel tipper which had found residence in Swadlincote, over in Derbyshire. It had been pensioned off and its bulk body had become a useful storage area for spare parts.

Another Scammell Routeman Mk III which came from the Blue Circle Cement fleet. It was seen here in an area of Kidsgrove known as Red Bull, where a dealer/breaker was based for a while. It is very likely to have been exported as parts or even a complete vehicle.

Luckily this E.R.F with LV cab got saved. It was parked here in an area of the old Shelton Steelworks before it went into preservation. The owner restored it to a high standard and actually used it to transport his vintage tractors.

Yet another Foden Haulmaster that found itself being used for storage; in this case it looks very much like a load of scrap has been deposited in the tipping body. This too was seen in Swadlincote.

Foden S80 vehicles were considered to be rather tough and many were sold as tippers rather than into general haulage. To find one that had been used as a refrigerated van was a little unusual. This six-wheeler was another down in Derbyshire, a long way from Kendal which is the name on the side of the van.

Now, this Atkinson had the tarpaulin pulled back to enable the photo to be taken. As it was a four-wheeler it might be safe to assume it was a genuine 'Raider' model, however experience has taught the author never to be sure and, in those days, not many notes were made; the photo taking preference!

E.R.F B Series. This eight-wheel lorry is fitted with a sleeper cab and also has a centrally mounted crane to facilitate the off-loading of bricks and blocks etc. It was seen in its owner's yard pending a decision on its ultimate fate.

A rather battered Foden S83 tractor unit seen on waste ground over in Lincolnshire. Gosberton Farm Produce (G.F.P) specialised in the provision of pre-packed vegetables using the 'Novapac' brand name and had used this as a yard shunter.

This K Series Dodge was spotted loaded on a trailer in South Yorks. It was probably waiting for its final trip to the scrapyard. The four-wheel tipper with drop sides had been with a Sheffield plant operator.

Spotted parked up in the old Ensor yard at Swadlincote, Derby, this E.R.F had at one time been one of the vehicles that operated with a trailer which had steering axles. The set up was useful for tight turns but unfortunately did incur an unladen weight penalty.

Parked in a Staffordshire fuel companies yard this A.E.C six-wheel tanker was actually still in use as a static bowser to store buffer stock. The Ergomatic cab is showing typical signs of the 'tin worm', something they unfortunately suffered from.

Typical of some operator's ingenuity, this Foden S39 'Sixer' was originally a concrete mixer. Having had the mixer equipment removed it had an 'Iron Fairy' crane mounted on the back to provide a useful vehicle to use around the yard.

This A.E.C Mercury was new to Grantham Road Services; it then went to Rowes of Tamworth who added a livestock body. It passed to an owner driver who used it on local cattle markets but when photographed it had been retired and the cattle float removed leaving it as a flat. The vehicle did pass into preservation.

The mainstay of many a fleet years ago was the combination of a Gardner engine, David Brown gearbox and Kirkstall axles. This Atkinson Borderer had the popular 6LXB 180 engine fitted and was from the fleet of Cannings from Leyland, Lancs. However here it had found its way to a dealer's yard in Lincolnshire quietly awaiting its fate.

The sad remains of an E.R.F 54G four-wheel flat platform lorry seen in a haulier's yard in Newark. Sometime during its life, it had been fitted with the later 'A Series' type grille giving it a more modern look.

This Leyland Super Comet of Plants from Tean, Staffs, was parked in a corner of their yard for a number of years before being bought for preservation. Fortunately, it was restored in its original livery by the Pyatt Brothers before it was sold on to another enthusiast.

'Newark Steel Flyer' is the name scribbled on the front of this E.R.F 5MW tractor unit seen suffering the ravages of time. The Motor Panels all steel cab was an 'off the peg' cab used in various forms by several vehicle manufacturers. This one was again seen in Newark, Notts, many years ago.

Found among several other vehicles that had come to the end of their working life was this E.R.F KV four-wheel flat. It was on a farm in Lincolnshire and with nature slowly taking over it presumably was not saved. The photo dates back to the early 1990s.

Right next to the E.R.F in the previous photo was this Volvo F88 tractor unit. At the time the cab had not suffered too bad from rust, something the F88 was prone to. The condition of this one would not have been beyond redemption.

This E.R.F eight-wheel tipper was actually purchased by a dealer and got exported to some far away distant shores for further use. It was in quite good condition and would not have taken too much effort to make it serviceable.

With the later style wider grille this F88 Volvo unit was again in the same location as the previous three photographs. At one time this would have been someone's pride and joy and had been adorned with the popular continental embellishment's like air horns, sun visor etc.

Still in the same Lincolnshire yard, this Austin K9 which was derived from the civilian Lodestar Series, was introduced in 1952 for military service as a 4 x 4 vehicle and had several body styles including radio signal vans, general service bodies etc. This one had retained much of its military features and had been used as a recovery vehicle for an Austin Dealership in Horncastle, Lincs.

Seen in a yard in Penistone, Yorkshire, was this Scammell Trunker 2 that had been in use with Flouch Transport, possibly on contract to Hepworth Pipes. By the time of the photograph it had been replaced by a Foden and was enjoying a more tranquil life in retirement.

Yet another Volvo F88 with the later wide grille that had seen better days. It was tucked up a corner of a Lincolnshire farm quietly waiting for nature to take its course, unless it was destined for the scrapyard!

Back to Penistone and again in Flouch Transport's yard was this Albion that had been on contract to Guinness and painted into their livery. Again, as the photograph was taken over thirty years ago it's not known if it survived.

I came across this venerable old Leyland Octopus recovery vehicle with the '22' cab in Chirk, North Wales. A few years later the vehicle had apparently been removed from here and had reputedly gone into the Liverpool area.

E.R.F tractor unit that was found again over in Lincolnshire. F.P. & R.A. Walter is the name on the headboard and the E letter has been broken. The vehicle has a Lincolnshire registration plate and the livery looks very much like the old Ind Coope brewery colours.

This Foden DG was one of the vehicles that resided for a number of years at the old established Foden Dealer – Sam Satterthwaite in Streetly close to Birmingham. Sam was old school and the photo was taken on occasion of his eightieth birthday celebration, also attended by a number of enthusiasts Foden vehicles.

Quite a number of these mobile cranes were built on Albion chassis, this example was seen in a commercial vehicle breakers yard where it was still in everyday use. The L.A.D. (Leyland, Albion, Dodge) cab on these were the long door version made by Motor Panels of Coventry.

The driveway of the long-gone and revered Midland Motors of Oadby in Leicestershire is the scene of this photo. Houses have been built here but many years ago access to the yard was straight forward. Typical of many such yards we can see a selection of vehicles that have given their best. They include an ex-B.R.S. Seddon artic with a couple of cabs on the trailer.

A rather beat up Atkinson Borderer that according to the badge had a Cummins engine fitted. The Borderer was a popular motor with many hauliers and was the last style of cab before the amalgamation with Oldham-based Seddon to form Seddon-Atkinson.

In the same yard as the previous photograph at Lostock Gralam, Northwich, was this Foden S40 tractor that had been on the fleet of Harris roadways. At the time of the picture the company had been absorbed into the Transport Development Group (T.D.G.). Fortunately the vehicle survived into preservation.

A grand old E.R.F 68GX, although seen as a chassis cab it had been used as a towing vehicle by Stamford, Lincolnshire-based C&G Concrete. The company ceased trading in 2011 so presumably the vehicle was scrapped.

Also at C&G Concrete was this Leyland Octopus 2 eight-wheel aggregate tipper. The yard contained a number of vehicles out of use, the majority being concrete mixers. As can be seen, vandals had managed to gain access and caused a lot of damage, later on the company even suffered an arson attack.

One of the many Leyland Bison six-wheel concrete mixers that were in the C&G yard at Stamford. Again, although complete when parked up it had suffered from the vandals, with most if not all the glass smashed.

John Lee Steel Services of Grantham were established in 1845 when the founder actually made fur felt hats! Myxomatosis put an end to that side of the business and they diversified into steel stockholding among other things, including road haulage. This Leyland Buffalo unit had certainly seen better days.

This Morris Commercial four-wheel drive vehicle is an ex-military machine that had seen use as a breakdown lorry. It was found hemmed in, languishing in a yard in Bourne, Lincolnshire, and judging by the look of it had been out of service for quite a while.

Another chassis cab, this time a Foden Haulmaster six-wheeler. The body had probably been removed, refurbished, and then placed onto a newer chassis. This would obviously be an economical option and was often carried out by many operators.

In quite good order this E.R.F 64GXB artic box van was in a Lincolnshire quarry and used as a store/workshop. But apparently on occasion it would have been moved in and around the quarry to service or repair plant and equipment.

It is not very clear just what we have here. The crane looks very much to be ex-military but the Ergomatic cab may have been a later addition. According to the badge it is off an A.E.C Mandator, which was, of course, a tractor unit.

In a very sorry state was this Leyland Marathon tractor unit seen quietly rusting away. The Marathon did find favour in a number of fleets and apparently gave good service. It was the forerunner of the equally popular T45 range Leyland Roadtrain.

As an enthusiast the author had for many years seen very plain green and red lorries on the road, with little or no clues to their origin. It was a delight to actually find the yard of John Dickinson. All was revealed! This E.R.F 64GXB had long been withdrawn from service but did sport a full livery.

Fitted with a rear-mounted HIAB crane, this 7LV cabbed E.R.F was another lorry parked, out of use, in John Dickinson's yard.

One of a number of retired Atkinson vehicles that resided in a Cornish dealership. The Guest Road Services Borderer with 180 Gardner 6LXB engine was another vehicle lucky enough to be saved and restored.

Austin FFK gulley emptier which was parked in an enthusiast's yard down near Launceston, Cornwall. The vehicle was purchased with a view to either restore or use for spares, but it did in fact get sold on.

And, I suppose, the final photograph should be of a vehicle that would have possibly been beyond any form of restoration. A genuine E.R.F A Series tractor unit which was tucked away on a farm in Dorset.